W9-COX-713

MAHATMA GANDHI

MAHATMA GANDHI

PROPONENT OF PEACE

by Sue Vander Hook

Content Consultant:
Ezra Rashkow, PhD
Lecturer, Department of History, University of Virginia

ABDO
Publishing Company

CREDITS

Published by ABDO Publishing Company, 8000 West 78th Street,
Edina, Minnesota 55439. Copyright © 2011 by Abdo Consulting
Group, Inc. International copyrights reserved in all countries. No
part of this book may be reproduced in any form without written
permission from the publisher. The Essential Library™ is a
trademark and logo of ABDO Publishing Company.

Printed in the United States of America,
North Mankato, Minnesota
052010
092010

 THIS BOOK CONTAINS AT LEAST 10% RECYCLED MATERIALS.

Editor: Mari Kesselring
Copy Editor: Sarah Frigon
Interior Design and Production: Kazuko Collins
Cover Design: Kazuko Collins

Library of Congress Cataloging-in-Publication Data
Vander Hook, Sue, 1949–
  Mahatma Gandhi : proponent of peace / Sue Vander Hook.
    p. cm. — (Essential lives)
  Includes bibliographical references and index.
  ISBN 978-1-61613-515-7
  1. Gandhi, Mahatma, 1869–1948—Juvenile literature.
2. Nationalists—India—Biography—Juvenile literature. 3.
Statesmen—India—Biography—Juvenile literature. 4. Pacifists—
India—Biography—Juvenile literature. 5. Nonviolence—India—
History—20th century—Juvenile literature. 6. India—Politics and
government—1919–1947—Juvenile literature. I. Title.
  DS481.G3V25 2011
  954.03′5092—dc22
  [B]
                                        2010000540

TABLE OF CONTENTS

Mahatma Gandhi, circa 1930

THE SALT MARCH

is name was Mohandas Karamchand
Gandhi, but people all over the world
called him Mahatma—the "Great Soul." To his
followers in India, he was Bapu—"Father" or "Father
of the Nation." Eventually, the world would know

him just as Gandhi, a remarkable man who quietly led an entire nation to independence.

Gandhi was a very small person, standing 5 feet 2 inches (157 cm) tall and weighing approximately 110 pounds (50 kg). Still, his influence was immeasurable. He could turn a quiet speech into a nationwide call to action. He could transform a peaceful walk into a powerful protest march. And he could hold up a small symbol, such as a handful of salt, and control an entire empire.

Dandi Today

The village of Dandi, the final destination of the Salt March, is now a popular tourist site and one of India's major salt centers. It is also a holy place for followers of Gandhi. Every year, people visit Dandi to pay homage to Gandhi and the people who sacrificed their lives for India's independence.

GATHERING SALT

The evening of April 6, 1930, 60-year-old Gandhi stood on the shore of the Arabian Sea and defied the British Empire. He was in the small village of Dandi on the western coast of India. Ceremoniously, he bent down and scooped up a mixture of sea salt and mud in his hand. Then he stood, turned, and slowly lifted his hand triumphantly above his head. Before him gathered a crowd of Indian residents who had beaten their drums and clanged their cymbals on what would become a historic march to the sea. Gandhi's actions were significant.

With salt in hand, Gandhi proclaimed, "With this, I am shaking the foundations of the British Empire."[1] People in the crowd began to voice their approval, softly at first, and then swelling to a loud roar. They shouted and cheered, optimistic and hopeful for their future.

But what power was there in a handful of salt? How could a march to the sea affect the powerful British Empire? For a long time, the British had ruled India and imposed harsh taxes on necessary items such as salt. According to law, Indians could only purchase government-manufactured salt. The salt was expensive, with an excessive tax that caused great hardship, especially for the poor. Salt was a necessity of life, especially in India, an arid country with scorching temperatures and minimal rainfall. Even the cattle and other animals needed plenty of salt to survive.

Gandhi ranked the need for salt with essentials such as air and water. He criticized the government for taxing an important commodity that nature provided in abundance. The Salt Tax had become

Gandhi and his followers illegally gathered salt from the seashore.

a symbol of Britain's power and its right to rule the people of India. Gandhi stated:

> *The tax constitutes . . . the most inhuman poll tax that ingenuity of man can devise . . . 2,400 per cent on sale price! What this means to the poor can hardly be imagined by us. . . . [I]f the people had freedom, they could pick up salt from the deposits made by the receding tides on the bountiful coast.* [2]

And that was just what Gandhi did.

STRUGGLE FOR INDEPENDENCE

Plans for the Salt March, as it came to be called, began three months earlier, in January 1930. Gandhi had worked for many years to gain independence for India. But now he was growing bolder. He called the struggle for independence a "battle of Right against Might."[3] He even referred to British rule as "a curse."[4] Gandhi and Jawaharlal Nehru, an Indian lawyer also committed to India's independence, wrote a statement to the British government on January 26, 1930:

> *The British Government in India has not only deprived the Indian people of their freedom but has based itself on the exploitation of the masses, and has ruined India economically, politically, culturally and spiritually. . . . We hold it to be a crime against men and God to submit any longer to a rule that has caused this fourfold disaster to our country.*[5]

The Salt Act of 1882

In 1882, the British enacted the Salt Act in India. The punishment section of the law read: "[A]ny person convicted of an [offense] under section 9, shall be punished with imprisonment. . . . [A]ll contraband salt, and every vessel, animal or conveyance used in carrying contraband salt shall be liable to confiscation . . . . [A]ny salt-revenue officer guilty of cowardice shall . . . be punished with imprisonment which may extend to three months."[6]

The statement was called the Purna Swaraj—India's Declaration of Independence. It was dangerous to publicly denounce the government, but Gandhi was compelled to speak out fearlessly.

Gandhi then presented the British with a list of reforms. He itemized what was required of the government to avoid civil disobedience by the people. One of his demands was that the government abolish the Salt Tax.

Satyagraha—Civil Disobedience

Nearly two months later, the British still had not ended the oppressive tax. Gandhi took action. On March 12, 1930, he and 78 of his followers began a 240-mile (386-km) journey

British Rule in India

British rule in India has a long history. In the early seventeenth century, the British began building trading posts in India—first in Surat in western India, and then on the eastern coast at Madras. In Madras, the British built their first major fort in approximately 1640. However, it was the establishment of Fort Williams in Calcutta, Bengal, that led to the first real British possession of India as a colony. The local Indian ruler of Calcutta was concerned that the British were strengthening their fortifications. He formed an army and drove the British out of the city. But the British returned to Calcutta. In the summer of 1757, Robert Clive led the British to a victory in the battle at Plassey through bribes and subterfuge, while hardly firing a shot. The British installed a puppet ruler who would protect their interests in Bengal. Clive became known as the "conqueror of India." This was the start of British control in India.

on foot to the Arabian Sea. They started at Gandhi's religious community dwelling, Sabarmati Ashram, and walked very slowly for 24 days, adding thousands of protesters from villages along the way.

Upon reaching the seaside village of Dandi on April 6, Gandhi committed a daring act—he stole salt from the shoreline. He had deliberately committed a crime, and he would willingly accept the punishment. In India, it was called *satyagraha* which means "civil disobedience" or "soul force." By scooping up salt, Gandhi and the people of India made the choice to no longer obey the government that had driven them into servitude and poverty.

In the coming months, the people quietly united for the cause of freedom that would transform India forever. And Gandhi—the Mahatma, their Bapu—would make a permanent mark on history. Without firing a shot or forming an army, Gandhi would shake up the British Empire and achieve *swaraj*—India's independence and freedom from foreign domination.

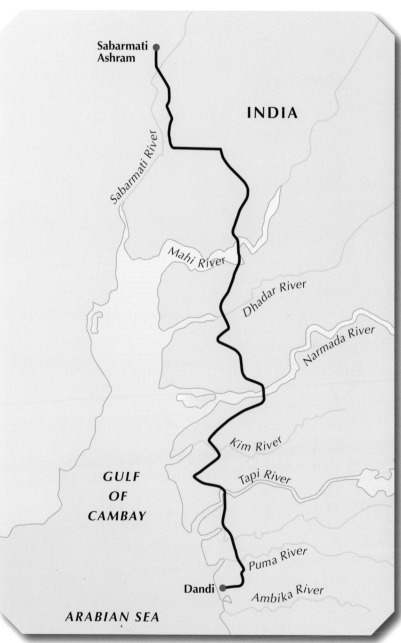

Sabarmati
Ashram

INDIA

Sabarmati River

Mahi River

Dhadar River

Narmada River

Kim River

GULF
OF
CAMBAY

Tapi River

Puma River

Dandi

Ambika River

ARABIAN SEA

This map shows the route of the Salt March.

Kashmir

British India

Indian States

Baluchistan

**Boundary of
Present-day India**

Rajputana

Porbandar

Burma

*ARABIAN
SEA*

Hyderabad

*BAY OF
BENGAL*

Mysore

Travancore

Ceylon

A map of India during the time of British rule

TIMID BEGINNINGS

Mohandas Karamchand Gandhi was born on October 2, 1869, in Porbandar, Gujarat, India. When Gandhi was born, Porbandar was an active harbor city, with the Arabian Sea on one side and beautiful mountains on the other.

Religious Upbringing

Mohandas was the fourth and youngest child of Karamchand and Putlibai Gandhi. His older siblings included a sister, Raliatbehn, and two brothers, Laxmidas and Karsandas. Other relatives and several servants lived with the Gandhis in their large three-story house.

Mohandas's father, Karamchand, was the *dewan*, or prime minister, of Porbandar. He had inherited the post from his own father. Although the Gandhis were part of the Vaisya caste, which consisted of merchants, they had acquired a political position. This was relatively common in Gujarat.

Every day, Karamchand took care of city affairs in the courtyard of the Krishna temple. He was a powerful man who settled legal matters, set property boundaries, and resolved family disputes. Mohandas later wrote that his father was "truthful, brave and generous, but short-tempered."[1] Karamchand was also a religious man, a Hindu, who worshipped often in the temple, listening to religious speeches and reciting prayers.

Putlibai was Karamchand's fourth wife. They had married when he was 40 and she was 13. Karamchand's first two wives had died. The third,

*Mohandas grew up following the Hindu religion.
He was devoted to the god Rama.*

who had been critically ill, gave him permission to
marry before she passed away.

Putlibai was a small, simple, religious woman who
followed the Vaishnava Pranami faith. This religion
combined elements of Islam into Hinduism,

particularly the rejection of idolatry. Her main focus, though, was worshipping God and praying every day, not following a religion or a set of complicated rituals. Mohandas later wrote:

> *The outstanding impression my mother . . . left on my memory is that of saintliness. She was deeply religious. . . . She would take the hardest vows and keep them without flinching.*[2]

Putlibai fasted regularly, either to please the gods or to attempt to make something happen. Once she refused to eat until the sun came out from behind the clouds. When the days remained cloudy, she said, "It does not matter. God does not want me to eat today."[3] Putlibai passed on her deep faith to her son, who learned to live a religious and modest lifestyle of charity, peace, and chastity. Meat, alcohol, tobacco, and drugs were prohibited.

TIMID BOY

Mohandas was a timid child who was especially afraid of the Krishna temple next door to his house. Everything there scared him—the smells, the dark rooms, and the chanting priests. He was also afraid of ghosts. The children's nurse, Rambha, once told him, "There are no ghosts, but if you are afraid, repeat the name of Rama."[4] Rama was the name of a Hindu god. Mohandas would remember this advice for the rest of his life.

Temple of Peace

Gandhi's childhood home in Porbandar is now a temple of peace known as Kirti Mandir. The original three-story house still stands. An ornately carved structure surrounds the house, rising 79 feet (24 m). This is symbolic of Gandhi's age, 79, when he died in 1948. The 79 lighted clay lamps arranged at the top of the memorial are also symbolic of his age. In accordance with Gandhi's equal tolerance for all religions, Kirti Mandir is not a temple to any one religion.

Under the dome are life-size portraits of Gandhi and his wife. Beneath the portraits are two words: truth and nonviolence. Twenty-eight marble pillars, each 12 feet (3.7 m) high, encircle a large open space. Inscribed on the pillars are Gandhi's principles, his speeches, and the main events of his life.

The rooms of the house are small, dark, and extremely hot in the summer. The top story, however, is open and bright with a good view of the city and harbor. The main floor now houses a library and reading room, a picture gallery, and a museum. On the second floor are rooms where members of the Gandhi family can stay. The airy third floor has a terrace with plants commemorating the potted flowers Gandhi watered as a child.

Mohandas rarely played with other children. He was quiet and preferred being alone. However, Mohandas was not an obedient child and often entertained himself with clever mischief. It was hard for Rambha to keep track of her adventurous, strong-willed charge.

But young Mohandas also had admirable qualities, such as his devotion to truth, nonviolence, and fairness. Even when it would have been easier to lie, he did not hesitate to tell the truth. If someone struck him or mistreated him, he refused to retaliate. When it came to sports, he was chosen as the umpire for his fair judgment.

Miserable School Years

Mohandas began school in Porbandar when he was six years old. A year later, his father accepted a position as chief *karbhari*, or adviser, of Rajkot, a smaller city approximately 120 miles (193 km) northwest of Porbandar. Karamchand took his oldest son, Laxmidas, with him and left the rest of the family at home. After two years, he sent for his family. They moved into a large house in Rajkot.

In Rajkot, nine-year-old Mohandas attended Taluka School. He was absent nearly half the time during his first year.

The Caste System

There are approximately 3,000 different castes in India. Caste in India often determines a person's lot in life—where they are positioned in the social hierarchy, what their profession will be, how they practice their religion, and who they associate with. In Gandhi's time, members of separate castes were not allowed to marry each other or even to eat with one another. There are four main original categories of castes:

- *Brahman*: priests and teachers
- *Kshatriya*: rulers and soldiers
- *Vaisya*: merchants and traders
- *Sudra*: laborers

There is a fifth caste called the *Panchamas*, although this term is rarely used. These are members of the lowest caste, also called "untouchables." As of 2001, approximately 16.2 percent of India's population belonged to this caste.

His schoolmates often teased him about his appearance. Most people thought he was an ugly child. He had huge protruding ears, a wide nose, beady black eyes, and a stick-like neck that seemed to struggle to support his head. He ran home every day after school, afraid to talk to anyone. The ridicule was relentless. Mohandas also struggled with his education, especially multiplication. "My intellect must have been sluggish, and my memory raw," he later claimed.[5] Mohandas would later recall his school days as the most miserable years of his life.

Growing Up

At the age of 11, Mohandas entered Kathiawar High School. He attended this school for seven years. Although still an average student, he was constantly thinking. It bothered him that many of his classes were taught in English. More than a

Arranged Marriages

For centuries, parents in India have arranged their children's marriages, including choosing a spouse and planning the wedding. However, as India modernizes, more couples are choosing love marriages. These are unions based on love and mutual attraction. Of course, parents' approval is still valued.

The British governors of India when Mohandas was a child, circá 1875

century of British rule had given rise to English
becoming the language of education.

Mohandas also began to question India's culture
and customs. He especially wondered about the
Indian caste system that divided people into rich
and poor according to who their family was. He saw
no reason why some people should be born inferior
to others.

As the years of his childhood passed, Mohandas grew more confident and independent. Even his appearance did not seem to affect him anymore. He enjoyed life, exploring everything around him and growing potted plants on the rooftop of his house.

When Mohandas was 13 years old and still in high school, his parents planned an event that would change his life forever. That year, he would marry a 13-year-old girl he had never met—a girl chosen by his parents to be his wife.

The exterior of the Gandhis' home in Porbandar

Mohandas Gandhi and his wife, Kasturbai, circa 1915

CHILD MARRIAGE

For a long time, it was the custom for parents in India to choose spouses for their children. When Mohandas was very young, his parents selected a girl for him. However, she died, and they had to choose someone else. When the second girl also died, they again found someone who would be a suitable mate for their son. Mohandas was approximately seven years old when his parents made an agreement with the parents of Kasturbai Makanji. Mohandas did not know Kasturbai, nor did he know about the betrothal. In fact, Mohandas and Kasturbai would not meet until their wedding day.

Chosen Spouse

Kasturbai was small in stature, like Mohandas. She lived in Porbandar with her parents, not far from the Gandhis. Her father was a successful businessman who dealt in grain, cotton, and cloth. Kasturbai was just a few months older than Mohandas.

In 1883, when Mohandas and Kasturbai were 13 years old, the parents on both sides began organizing their children's wedding. In May, the festivities began. Guests donned their finest clothes and jewelry to attend events with the best food and most talented musicians money could buy.

A wedding was an elaborate, expensive affair. Because of the cost, the Gandhis made this wedding a triple ceremony. Mohandas and Kasturbai would be married, and so would Karsandas, Mohandas's older brother. The third marriage would be Mohandas's cousin.

The ceremony took place in Porbandar. Mohandas's father had stayed in Rajkot until it was time for the ceremony and then made the journey by stagecoach. However, close to Porbandar, his carriage overturned. He was seriously injured, but the wedding could not be postponed. He arrived, heavily wrapped in bandages, and took part in the ceremony.

Seven Vows of Marriage

At a Hindu wedding ceremony, the bride and groom take seven steps. They make the following vows for each step:

1. To provide a prospered living for the household or the family that they will look after and avoid those that might hinder their healthy living.

2. To develop their physical, mental, and spiritual powers in order to lead a lifestyle that will be healthy.

3. To earn a living and increase by righteous and proper means, so that their materialistic wealth increases manifold.

4. To acquire knowledge, happiness, and harmony by mutual love, respect, understanding, and faith.

5. To expand their heredity by having children, for whom they will be responsible, and to pray to be blessed with healthy, honest, and brave children.

6. For self-control of the mind, body, and soul, and longevity of their marital relationship.

7. To be true and loyal to each other and remain companions and best friends for a lifetime.[1]

Seven Vows

It was a solemn ceremony. The bride and groom sat on a special platform while a Hindu priest performed the appropriate chants and speeches. Then, the couple stood and performed the *Saptapadi*—the seven steps symbolic of the seven vows of marriage. In their vows, they promised faithfulness, devotion, and respect. In the last vow, they promised to stay together for the rest of their lives. Mohandas and Kasturbai would indeed fulfill that vow.

Mohandas and Kasturbai came to love each other and remained devoted to the end. However, Mohandas would always look back on his childhood marriage with disapproval. He would later comment, "I can see no moral argument in support of such a preposterously early marriage."[2]

With the triple wedding behind them, the Gandhis returned to Rajkot. Mohandas took his new bride with him and returned to Kathiawar High School. However, Mohandas had a difficult school year. He

Child Marriages

In modern India, the Child Marriage Restraint Act states that a girl must be 18 and a boy 21 before they can marry. However, the law is routinely ignored. Every spring, hundreds of mass marriage ceremonies take place in which girls under 18 and as young as 4 are wed and move immediately to their husbands' homes.

attended only one-third of the days and did not show up for the final exam. But somehow he convinced school officials to let him go on to the next level. He promised them he would have great success if they would only let him advance.

His scores did improve dramatically the following year, although he still struggled with English. At the end of the year, Mohandas passed the final exam, ranking third in his class of 40 boys. However, success turned to sorrow for Mohandas. In 1885, at the age of 16, he experienced two of the most traumatic events of his life. In November, his father died, probably the result of his injuries sustained in the carriage accident. Several weeks later, Kasturbai gave birth to their first child. But the baby lived only three or four days. For the rest of his life, Mohandas would be troubled by thoughts of death.

Life's Direction

In 1887, 17-year-old Mohandas finished high school. In January 1888, he entered Samaldas College, approximately 90 miles (145 km) southeast of Rajkot. College overwhelmed him. He missed Kasturbai and his family. His grades plummeted, and after five months, he dropped out and returned

Young Mohandas

to Rajkot. While he was gone, Kasturbai had given birth to a son. They named him Harilal.

Mohandas had failed miserably at school. His family was concerned. Mohandas sought counsel from Mavji Dave, a Brahmin priest and the family's longtime friend and counselor. The priest advised Mohandas to follow in his father's footsteps and become the dewan of Rajkot. But since it was no longer possible to inherit a government position, Mohandas would have to go to school in London, England, and get a law degree. It would be a very costly venture and he would have to leave his wife and son behind.

Hurdles

Mavji Dave's son, who had studied law in England, warned Mohandas about London. He told him he would have to eat meat, drink alcohol, and spend a lot of money. He also would most likely give in to the many temptations that lurked everywhere. This went completely against Mohandas's religious beliefs, and he became very depressed.

Mohandas's mother was also concerned that Mohandas would violate his religious beliefs in England. And, Mohandas needed his mother's permission to go. In the end, Mohandas made a solemn vow before a monk. He vowed not to touch wine, women, or meat while in England. Satisfied, Mohandas's mother then gave permission for her son's trip. His brother Laxmidas gave up his share of the family estate to help finance Mohandas's education. Finally, there were no more hurdles, and Mohandas made plans for his journey.

London and Law School

In September 1888, Mohandas arrived in London. Right away, he knew he did not fit in. The British dressed differently, served food he did not like, and addressed each other in their own unique way. Alone in his hotel room, he wept and longed to go home. But he had committed to three years. He had to stay.

Dr. Pranjivan Mehta, a friend of the family, was his connection in London. Mehta arranged for him to live with Shukla Saheb, another law student, for one month. Saheb's job was to teach Mohandas English customs and make sure he always spoke the English language. But Saheb also pressured Mohandas to eat meat. Mohandas refused and ate only oatmeal for breakfast, and bread, jam, and spinach for both lunch and dinner. Saheb asked, "What is the value of a vow made before an illiterate mother, and in ignorance of conditions here?"[3] Mohandas said, "A vow is a vow. It cannot be

The Vegetarian Society

While living in London, Mohandas joined the Vegetarian Society. It was at the society's meetings that Mohandas gained confidence to speak in public. Established in 1847, the society promotes a lifestyle of no meat, poultry, or fish. A vegetarian's diet consists of vegetables, fruits, grains, nuts, seeds, and sometimes dairy products.

broken."[4] After that, Saheb did not argue with him anymore.

Mohandas then moved in with a family in London. The mother, a widow, tried to cook vegetarian meals for him, but nevertheless, he was always hungry. Finally, he found a vegetarian restaurant and ate his first filling meal since he had arrived. After that, he ate there often. He also proclaimed himself a vegetarian and joined the Vegetarian Society.

Mohandas was a diligent student, although his struggle with the English language made school more challenging. At first, he resisted English customs and dress and tried to maintain his Indian traditions. But sometime in the spring of 1889, he began dressing like a fine English gentleman. He donned a shiny top hat, a fine shirt, and striped pants. He wore a colorful tie, a double-breasted vest, and a formal coat. His shoes were shiny patent leather, and over them he wore leather spats.

In 1891, Mohandas Gandhi finished law school and passed the bar examination. He was now a barrister—a lawyer. London had been a difficult, lonely experience for him, and he was ready to return to India.

Gandhi studied law in London, England.

Gandhi, center, worked at a law firm in South Africa.

THE PAIN OF PREJUDICE

When Mohandas Gandhi arrived home
to India in 1891 he was greeted with
disturbing news. Just weeks before he arrived,
his mother had died. Gandhi was shocked and
devastated. But he shed no tears and went on with

life as though nothing had happened. Inside, however, he was in turmoil. He turned to Shrimad Raychandbhai, an Indian philosopher, for advice and friendship.

Gandhi's family expected that Gandhi would immediately start a law practice in Rajkot. However, in London, Gandhi had studied British law. He needed to learn the Indian judicial system. For several months, he attended court hearings at the High Court in Bombay. He had little interest in the cases, however, and often dozed off in the courtroom. Upon his return to Rajkot, he set up a small law practice, but it proved to be exasperating as well as unsuccessful.

To South Africa

Meanwhile, a law firm in South Africa asked Gandhi to represent a wealthy Indian merchant there. They would need him for a year and would pay his fare, living expenses, and salary. Gandhi could hardly refuse this new opportunity and a chance to finally support his growing family. He now had two sons. The second son, Manilal, had been born the year after he returned to India.

In April 1893, 23-year-old Gandhi set sail for
the east coast of South Africa. He arrived in Durban
but soon traveled north to Pretoria. What he was
about to experience would change the course of
his life. South Africa was a sharply divided nation.
Blacks, whites, and Indians were judged by the color
of their skin, their religion, their occupation, and
their class. All of these groups were in conflict with
each other, and the white community was divided
against itself. The Indians, who had been brought
to work in the sugarcane fields, were detested most.
They were indentured laborers, which meant that
they worked in exchange for transportation, land,
or other necessities. People called them "coolies" or
"samis," offensive terms for unskilled laborers.

TROUBLE ON THE TRAIN

It was a long, roundabout ride to Pretoria. On
the first leg of his journey, Gandhi traveled by train,
first class. On board, a servant reported him to a
railroad official. People of color were not allowed
in the first-class section. When the official ordered
him to third class, Gandhi refused because he had
a first-class ticket. The man insisted he get off the
train or he would call the police. At the next station,

a policeman threw Gandhi and his luggage off
the train. Gandhi waited all night in the cold and
pondered his options. Should he go back to India?
Should he fight back against this racial injustice? He
decided to stay.

The next day, Gandhi explained
what happened in a telegram to
the manager of the railway. On the
next leg of his journey, Gandhi was
allowed to ride in first class. Finally,
he boarded a stagecoach. People of
color could not sit with white people,
so Gandhi was ordered to sit with
the driver. But when a white man
wanted that seat, Gandhi was ordered
to sit on the floor. When Gandhi
protested, the man assaulted him and
tried to push him off the coach. At
the insistence of the white passengers,
Gandhi was allowed to sit inside.
The next day, Gandhi reported the
incident to the coach company, which
assured him he would not be attacked
again.

The Plague in India

During Gandhi's return
to India for six months in
1896, the bubonic plague
broke out in Bombay.
He volunteered his ser-
vices, inspecting and
cleaning bathrooms in
homes and businesses
throughout the city to
keep the plague from
spreading.

ALL RELIGIONS

By the time Gandhi arrived in Pretoria, he was determined to fight for equal rights. During the first week, he met with a group of Indian merchants—Hindus and Muslims alike—to discuss the Indian condition. His speech encouraged them to live a life that was truthful and clean, and to put aside their divisions over religion and caste. It was his first of many public speeches.

Gandhi worked with people of all races and religions. He met with Hindus, Muslims, Christians, Jews,

Divided South Africa

For hundreds of years, South Africa was a racially divided country. In the late eighteenth century, when the British took control of the Cape of Good Hope, the colony had as many as 25,000 slaves and 20,000 white colonists. The whites ruled the colony, and people were separated according to race and class. Although slavery was abolished in 1834, racial tensions grew over inequality and prejudice.

The conflict intensified after 1869, when diamond mines were discovered near Kimberley. Britain quickly claimed the area and brought in hordes of black and Indian laborers to work the mines. By 1899, when Gandhi was in South Africa, racial tensions between the British and the Boers, white Dutch farmers, had escalated to war—the Boer War. Approximately 500,000 British soldiers fought 65,000 Boers. Black South Africans were pulled into the conflict on both sides. The British imprisoned both Boers and blacks in racially separate concentration camps, where many people died in dreadful conditions. The war ended in 1902. However, the apartheid government, which separated people by race and offered limited opportunities to nonwhites, ruled from 1948 to 1994. Racial conflicts continue to this day.

Sikhs, Jains, and Buddhists. He studied their religions with an open mind. However, some strict Hindus hated him for accepting other religions.

Deciding to Stay

In 1894, when Gandhi's one-year commitment was up, he prepared to return to India. About that time, the British government in South Africa passed several new bills that forced Indians to return to India or forever become serfs, members of the lowest class. These bills also forbade Indians from voting, farming, or owning property. They imposed heavy taxes on each family member. Indians also had to carry passes to appear on public streets. Violators were arrested and put in prison. Gandhi decided to stay in South Africa to object to the laws and organize opposition.

Gandhi wrote to government officials, delivered passionate speeches, and published newspaper articles and pamphlets. He encouraged Indians not to pay the taxes or carry passes. Many were arrested for disobeying the government.

In 1896, Gandhi, now 27, returned to India to pack up his house and bring his family to South Africa. In December, Gandhi returned with his wife, two sons—now nine and five years old—and his ten-year-old niece. The following year, the Gandhis had a third son, Ramdas. Their last son, Devdas, would be born in 1900.

THE SIMPLE LIFE

Gandhi now set out to simplify his life. His family did their own laundry. They also cut their own hair, since most barbers would not serve people with dark skin. And Gandhi volunteered two or three hours a day at a small hospital. He also resumed his campaign against racial injustice. When a bitter civil war—the Boer War—broke out in 1899, Gandhi organized and trained Indians to help. He ran an ambulance service that was willing to treat people no one else would touch.

In 1904, Gandhi simplified his life even more. He followed a Jain principle called *aparigraha*, or limiting possessions only to what is necessary. He rejected fine clothes, jewelry, and a nice house. He established an ashram, a simple religious communal farm, near Durban. There, his family and friends of many different religions lived a simple, shared lifestyle.

Gandhi was preoccupied with self-control and self-denial, which he believed would lead to union with God. He fasted regularly. Then, Gandhi decided to follow *brahmacharya*, a Hindu vow to control all his senses at all times. It included abstinence from all sexual activity. Gandhi wanted to be selfless and free of all physical desires. Later in his life, Gandhi admitted to sleeping naked with a few women to prove his strength of brahmacharya. Some of his followers found this behavior dishonorable.

THE BLACK ACT

By 1907, injustices against the Indian community were widespread. In March, the government passed the Asiatic Registration Act, commonly known as the Black Act. The law required Indians to be fingerprinted and to carry registration documents with them at all times. In another ruling, Indian marriages were declared invalid. Christian unions were the only marriages the government considered legal.

Joy in Serving

Gandhi delighted in helping other people. He wrote, "Service which is rendered without joy helps neither the servant nor the served. But all other pleasures and possessions pale into nothingness before service which is rendered in a spirit of joy."[1]

Gandhi began to develop the strategy of nonviolent civil disobedience that he would later call satyagraha. At a mass meeting of Indians in Pretoria, he announced his commitment to ignore the Black Act. He asked the Indian people to join him and fight for freedom. But he asked them to protest without violence or retaliation.

Gandhi and his followers refused to obey the Black Act. Workers went on strike, crippling the South African economy. Thousands of Indians also refused to register or carry their passes. They broke another law by going across South Africa's northwestern Transvaal border. Thousands were jailed for their disobedience, including Gandhi. However, Gandhi was thankful for his time in jail, where he could read and think in quiet.

In 1914, Gandhi's protests, speeches, and satyagraha paid off. South Africa again allowed Indians to vote. The burdensome tax was greatly reduced, and the government again recognized Indian marriages. Now, after 21 years in South Africa, Gandhi focused on another country—his homeland, India. There, he would continue to fight for justice and equality for the Indian people.

*Troops march during the Boer War. Gandhi was
in South Africa during this war.*

Gandhi's home in the ashram near Ahmedabad, India

MASSACRE AT AMRITSAR

In January 1915, 45-year-old Mohandas Gandhi arrived in India with his wife and four sons. Huge crowds welcomed him and cheered his arrival. He had become a national hero for what he had accomplished for the Indian people in South

Africa. Now, the people of India hoped he would do the same for them. Leaders of the Indian National Congress (INC), a nationalist political organization that led India's independence movement, suggested that Gandhi travel through India to reacquaint himself with the country before engaging in politics.

So, Gandhi traveled by train throughout India, visiting many of the country's 700,000 villages. He was particularly concerned about the living conditions of the untouchables, the lowest and most despised caste. In the cities, crowds gathered to hear him speak, and journalists eagerly interviewed him about his nonviolent cause. Wherever Gandhi went, crowds enthusiastically welcomed him as the leader they believed would set them free from oppression.

The Situation in India

At the time when Gandhi finally arrived in his home country, the situation in India was ripe for change. Most Indians were unhappy with British rule. They were fed up with their lack of participation in a government that controlled their daily lives.

In the late 1800s, British rule had done some good things for India. The government had built an

Indian railroad. They had created postal, telephone, and telegraph systems in the country. They even opened universities.

However, the British did not spend much money on the education of young Indian children. And despite the gains the British provided, many people still lived in poverty. Indians were not allowed the same job opportunities as British people. They could not hold important positions in the government or military. The British crushed any Indian rebellions with violence, manipulation, or bribery. The Indians did not trust the British and viewed the government's actions with great suspicion.

But India was important to the British and they would not give it up easily. The British government made money from Indian exports such as cotton cloth made by Indian weavers. The British also imposed high taxes

Indian National Congress

The Indian National Congress (INC), or Congress Party, is now India's dominant political party. Founded in 1885, the party was not opposed to British rule at first. As time went on, members became more strongly in favor of independence. Since 1948, six of India's prime ministers have been members of the Congress Party, including Jawaharlal Nehru and Indira Gandhi.

on products such as salt, which Indian citizens were forced to pay. The money the British made from India was not always used to develop India. Instead, much of the money was sent to England. Revenue from India was important to the British government.

ANOTHER ASHRAM

In 1914, World War I began, and the British government sought Gandhi's help. Although Gandhi was a pacifist, he rallied volunteers to serve in Britain's army. He believed that since Indians received the benefits and protection of the British Empire, they should support its military. Some people felt that Gandhi's assistance during the war conflicted with his belief in nonviolent protest.

In May 1915, Gandhi established another ashram, the Satyagraha Ashram at Kochrab. In June,

Satyagraha

Satyagraha is a word Gandhi created. It is derived from two Sanskrit words: *satya*, which means "truth," and *agraha*, which means "holding firmly to." Gandhi said, "Truth (*satya*) implies love, and Firmness (*agraha*) engenders and therefore serves as a synonym for force. I thus began to call the Indian movement 'satyagraha'; that is to say, the Force which is born of truth and love or nonviolence."[1]

he moved it to the banks of the River Sabarmati near the city of Ahmedabad. There, in the huddle of several huts, he instructed his followers in prayer, truth, nonviolent resistance, and self-denial. Eventually, this following grew to 230 people. Together, they lived simply, abstained from meat, and sometimes fasted. Gandhi even accepted an untouchable family into the commune. Other residents struggled to accept them, but Gandhi stood firm in his love for all people, regardless of caste.

The Sabarmati Ashram Today

Gandhi's ashram on the River Sabarmati in India is now a museum that collects and preserves Gandhi's writings, his possessions, and photographs of him. Exhibits include highlights of Gandhi's life and literature. The museum also studies and researches Gandhi's teachings and philosophies and observes events connected to Gandhi's life.

STRIKES AND RIOTS

Gandhi and the Indians who served in the military believed their service would earn them equality and more freedom, but it did not. At the end of the war, Gandhi was upset with the British government and proclaimed a *hartal*—a strike. The idea spread throughout India,

Many Indians fought for the British during World War I.
These Indian soldiers fought in Orleans, France.

and massive numbers of people participated. On
March 30, 1919, Indians shut down their stores and
refused to work. India's economy came to a halt, and
the Indian people realized they had power.

In Delhi and other large Indian cities, the strike turned into riots. Gandhi was appalled by the violence and called an end to the strike. He resolved to teach his people appropriate satyagraha, how to protest without fighting. He also fasted for three days, a sort of penance or self-punishment for the violence he had indirectly set in motion.

But discontent had already been sown, and the British government reacted with the Rowlatt Act which became a law on March 18, 1919. It gave the British power to suppress any hint of rebellion. Government authorities could silence the press, arrest protesters without a warrant, and hold protesters without trial. The Indian people were outraged. Among the most infuriated was Gandhi, who called for a protest. In April, Indians responded. They disrupted communication systems and railroads. Tens of thousands converged in silent, nonviolent protest in towns and cities throughout India.

THE AMRITSAR BLOODBATH

In April, in the northern city of Amritsar, approximately 5,000 Indians gathered at the Jallianwala Bagh Garden. It was a common gathering

*British Brigadier General Reginald Dyer led
the British troops at Amritsar.*

spot for sizeable crowds and consisted of a large
piece of land surrounded on three sides by walls and
buildings. On April 10, the British military fired on
the crowd, killing several dissenters.

The shootings triggered a chain of violence.
Some Indians set fire to government buildings and
the railroad station. The mob killed five British

citizens. The British fired on the crowd again and killed approximately 20 people. Over the next two days, the government banned assemblies of more than four people.

However, on April 13, thousands of Indians—men, women, and children—again met peacefully at Jallianwala Bagh in defiance of the ban. At approximately 5:30 p.m., British Brigadier General Reginald Dyer marched 90 troops into the area through a narrow entrance. Without any warning to the Indians gathered there, he ordered his soldiers to open fire. Hundreds were killed by gunfire, and many jumped into a nearby well to their deaths. Others were slaughtered as they tried to escape through narrow gates or climb walls. Some were crushed in the stampede of frightened protesters. The British recorded 379 killed and 200 injured, although others claimed hundreds more deaths.

The Butcher of Amritsar

Brigadier General Reginald Dyer's actions at the Amritsar massacre earned him the nickname "The Butcher of Amritsar." The Hunter Report, an investigation into the incident, concluded, "In continuing to fire for so long as he did it appears to us that General Dyer committed a grave error."[2] He was forced to resign from the army. However, Dyer had many British supporters who agreed with what he had done. In 1921, Dyer was stricken with paralysis and died in England on July 23, 1927.

One eyewitness recalled:

Corpses were lying all over. There were some wounded also. My estimate of the persons I saw lying was 1,500. . . . At several places, the corpses were ten or twelve thick. I saw some children lying dead.[3]

Gandhi regretted his failed plan of satyagraha. He said,

I am sorry that when I embarked upon a mass movement I underrated the forces of evil, and I must now pause and consider how best to meet the situation.[4]

INTERNATIONAL REACTION TO AMRITSAR

News of the bloodbath spread. Dyer justified

Amritsar Memorial

On April 13, 1961, the tall, oval-shaped Amritsar Memorial designed by Benjamin Polk was unveiled. Built in the Jallianwala Bagh Garden at Amritsar, the memorial commemorated the Indians who lost their lives in the massacre.

The surrounding walls and buildings still bear the holes from the bullets that slaughtered hundreds of the quiet protesters. The well that people jumped into to try to escape the barrage of bullets is also part of the memorial as is a flame that was later added to the site. A plaque where Dyer's troops opened fire states in capital letters, "This place is saturated with the blood of about 2,000 Hindu, Sikh and Muslim patriots who were martyred in a nonviolent struggle to free India from British domination."[5]

In 1997, Britain's Queen Elizabeth II visited the site to pay homage to the 1919 victims. She placed a wreath at the memorial, paused, and bowed her head. However, the trip was tainted by a comment made by her husband, Prince Philip. He remarked that the number of casualties was "vastly exaggerated."[6]

the attack, reporting that he had been attacked by a revolutionary army. He admitted he had not helped the wounded after the firing ended. "It was not my job," he said. "The hospitals were open and the medical officers were there. The wounded only had to apply for help."[7]

The events of April 1919 changed the people of India and intensified their opposition against the British. The massacre of April 13 was reported around the world and attracted a great deal of attention. Some British were ashamed of Dyer's actions, but overall they condoned them. The Indians were deeply humiliated and became afraid to protest. But they were also encouraged by one man—Mahatma Gandhi—who would now stand up even more boldly for his people in the face of the largest empire in the world. ⌐

The Amritsar Memorial

Untouchables in India, such as this family, lived in horrible conditions. Gandhi wanted the INC to end untouchability.

HOMESPUN

The Amritsar massacre was a turning point in Gandhi's life. For the first time, he believed the British government must be overthrown completely. Britain must leave India. In 1920, Gandhi became president of the All India Home

Rule League, an organization focused on swaraj—
India's independence and self-government.

INDIAN NATIONAL CONGRESS

Later that year, Gandhi wrote to the viceroy,
head of India's British government, "I have advised
my [Muslim] friends to withdraw their support
from Your Excellency's Government, and advised
the Hindus to join them."[1] The viceroy responded
that it was "the most foolish of all foolish schemes."[2]
Gandhi was not deterred and announced that
noncooperation would begin on August 1, 1920. He
declared July 31 to be a day of fasting and prayer.

In December, the INC met at Nagpur.
Approximately 20,000 people attended, including
some of India's poorest citizens. Gandhi emerged
as a passionate leader who could motivate the crowd
to action. People were immediately moved by his
courage, self-confidence, humor, and winsome
smile.

HOMESPUN CLOTHES

Delegates at the meeting passed resolutions to
eradicate untouchability and to spin and weave all
their own cloth. It was an act of defiance, a boycott of

Untouchables

At the turn of the twenty-first century, more than 160 million people in India are part of the lowest caste system, untouchables, or *Dalits*. Most of them are illiterate. These people are often considered less than human. They suffer many abuses, such as being beaten, murdered, lynched, raped, or burned alive.

As of 2010, a grassroots human rights movement was underway to demand rights for India's untouchables. In 2002, the United Nations Committee for the Elimination of Racial Discrimination passed a resolution denouncing the caste system. However, many Hindus were bothered by this, insisting that caste is not equivalent to race.

British-made cloth. Indians walked away from their British jobs, and lawyers no longer entered British courts. Two of those lawyers were Motilal Nehru and his son Jawaharlal Nehru, who would one day be India's first prime minister.

Thousands of students left the universities to fight for swaraj. They went to the villages to teach peasants how to read and engage in noncooperation. The country's peasants and working class stopped paying taxes and quit drinking alcohol, a high-profit item for the British.

For seven months, Gandhi traveled throughout India, speaking to crowds that were growing into massive assemblies. He encouraged people to give up everything British, including their clothing. He asked them to take off their British- or foreign-made clothes and pile them into a heap. Then, he set fire to them. He told the crowds they must learn to spin and weave their own cloth. It was a way to stop money from flowing to the British. It was also a way for the Indian people to become self-sufficient. For Gandhi, spinning was a spiritual act. He felt that it allowed a person's mind to focus on God.

Every day for at least half an hour, Gandhi spun thread with a small collapsible spinning wheel—a *charakha*—that he carried with him wherever he went. To the rhythm of the charakha he chanted, "Rama, Rama, Rama, Rama," which means "God, God, God, God." Spinning had become his passion and a symbol of his calling. Before long, nearly every Indian owned a small spinning wheel and made his or her own cloth, called *khadi* or homespun. The spinning wheel became an icon of civil disobedience and a symbol of courage.

Most people did not dare to enter Gandhi's presence unless they were wearing homespun clothes. Gandhi

Modern Homespun

The white homespun, or khadi, look of Gandhi's day has remained in fashion in India. The look often goes hand-in-hand with political statements or campaigns. Local handmade cloth still symbolizes self-respect and independence. Some shopkeepers still tout their products as locally made, selling nothing foreign or imported.

Gandhi felt that spinning was a spiritual act.

had long ago shed his fancy European clothes and
simplified his dress to a mere loincloth. He did not
want to be a replica of British or other European
culture. He was defying the government, but he was
also identifying with India's poor. Everywhere he
went, even when meeting with political leaders, he
wore only a loincloth and sometimes a shawl.

ANGRY MOB

In October 1921, the INC called for every Indian to break ties with the government. The British government reacted, arresting and jailing hundreds of Indian leaders. By the end of January 1922, approximately 30,000 Indians were jailed. Some Indians wanted open rebellion, but Gandhi was still committed to a peaceful revolution. "Nonviolence is the law of our species as violence is the law of the brute," he said.[3]

However, not all Indians could restrain themselves from violent retaliation. On February 5, 1922, an Indian mob set fire to a police station in Chaura. When people fled the building, the mob murdered them and threw their bodies into the fire. Gandhi was terribly disturbed by the incident and suspended the movement. He also fasted for five days for what the mob had done and as a plea for his people to end the violence.

The *Dhoti*

The loincloth Gandhi wore was a customary men's garment in India. The *dhoti*, as it was called, was a long, rectangular piece of unstitched cloth that was wrapped through the legs and around the waist. Gandhi wore a dhoti to identify with the poorest people in India.

"If I Am Arrested"

On March 10, the British had Gandhi arrested. They feared that his nonviolent message was just a cover for eventual violent revolution. Gandhi went to jail cheerfully, singing a hymn. The British expected Indians to be outraged and react at the arrest of their leader. But there were no outbreaks of violence. Gandhi had prepared his people for his arrest. In the *Young India*, a weekly journal, he had written several articles to teach people how to react if he were arrested. In one article titled

---

Family Relations

Gandhi was always loving and tolerant with residents of his ashram and the people of India. But his relationships with his wife and children were often tense. He could be very harsh with Kasturbai and cold toward his sons. His oldest, Harilal, suffered the most from his father's disapproval and eventual rejection. Likely in an effort to harm his father, he turned to alcohol and converted to Islam.

Kasturbai one day wrote Harilal a letter, begging him to get his life in order. She asked him to respect his father's commitment to purity and good conduct. However, Harilal brought further disgrace on his father when he established a fake business and took money from unsuspecting investors. When Gandhi received a letter about the scam, he published it in the *Young India*. He admitted that he was Harilal's father and explained that their values were very different. He blamed his son's shortcomings on Harilal's desire to get rich quickly. Gandhi admitted that he did not like how his son lived, but he loved Harilal regardless. "Men may be good," Gandhi wrote, "not necessarily their children."[4] Later, in a letter to his brother, Gandhi wrote that he no longer considered Harilal to be his son.

"If I Am Arrested," he wrote,

> *Rivers of bloodshed by the government*
> *cannot frighten me, but I should be deeply*
> *pained even if the people did so much as*
> *abuse the government for my sake or in*
> *my name.*[5]

On March 18, 1922, Gandhi
was tried at what came to be called
the Great Trial. He refused to be
represented by a lawyer and pleaded
guilty to all charges. He made a
lengthy statement, saying in part, "I
hold it an honor to be [rebellious]
towards a government which . . .
has done more harm to India than
any previous system."[6] The judge
gave Gandhi the maximum six-year
sentence. Gandhi went to prison with
a smile.

The people of India were upset
that their leader—the man they called
Mahatma and Bapu—was in prison.
But Gandhi was content in his cell.
He prayed, read, and spun on his

"You must not lose faith
in humanity. Humanity is
an ocean; if a few drops
of the ocean are dirty, the
ocean does not become
dirty."[7]

—*Gandhi*

wheel. He would be released two years later for an emergency appendectomy. Then, he would pick up satyagraha where he had left off. And he would face some of the most difficult obstacles yet to realizing an independent India.

A portrait of Gandhi, circa 1922

Chapter
7

Mahatma Gandhi and Sarojini Naidu walk during the Salt March.

THE POWER OF SALT

*I*t was 1924 when Gandhi recovered from his surgery. In his absence, satyagraha had subsided. Indians were back to life as usual. Any progress Gandhi had made had vanished. He was especially troubled that old divisions between Hindus and Muslims had reemerged. He went on a 21-day fast, proclaiming:

> *The struggle must for the moment be transferred to a change of heart among the Hindus and the [Muslims]. . . . [T]hey must be brave enough to love one another, to tolerate one another's religion, even prejudices and superstitions, and to trust one another.*[1]

When he broke his fast, Gandhi asked for the opening verses of the Koran to be read. He also wanted two hymns sung: a Hindu hymn and the Christian hymn, "When I Survey the Wondrous Cross."

ASHRAM LIFE

Meanwhile, Gandhi quietly returned to the ashram, where he read, wrote, and spun every day. He interacted with the diverse residents of the ashram, instructing them in cleanliness, work ethic, economizing, and spinning. He was particularly close to some of his followers. One was Madeleine Slade, daughter of British Rear-Admiral Sir Edmond Slade. She left England in 1925 to dedicate her life to Gandhi's principles and the struggle for India's independence. Gandhi gave her a new name—Mirabehn—and referred to her as his daughter.

Gandhi still wanted to challenge the British Empire, but he did not consider this the time to do it. The British and the rest of the world were still recovering from World War I. On December 26, 1924, Gandhi became president of the INC. He also worked on religious unity, wove homespun cloth, and helped the untouchables.

CAMPAIGN FOR INDEPENDENCE

In 1929, 60-year-old Gandhi aggressively revived his campaign for India's independence. This time, the effort was widespread. The protests and strikes were huge. Gandhi urged his followers to break the law and get arrested. If beaten, they were not to strike back. They were not to pay taxes, and they were urged to quit their government positions. In all they did, the people were to have dignity, discipline, and restraint. What would follow, Gandhi promised, would be self-respect and freedom.

On January 26, 1930, the INC issued Purna Swaraj, India's Declaration of Independence. On March 2, Gandhi sent a long letter to the viceroy. He accused the British government of degrading

India to servitude. He also asked for the Salt Act to be repealed. If it was not, he would disobey the law—without violence, of course. The viceroy responded with a short reply:

> *His Excellency . . . regrets to learn that you contemplate a course of action which is clearly bound to involve violation of the law and danger to the public peace.*[2]

TREK TO THE SEA

On the morning of March 12, 1930, Gandhi left his ashram with 78 followers and several reporters. They began their

History of Civil Disobedience

Gandhi and his followers taking salt from the sea is an example of civil disobedience. However, Gandhi was not the first person to use this kind of protest and he would not be the last. Civil disobedience was first practiced by religious groups hundreds of years ago. In 1200, Christian Saint Thomas Aquinas felt that it was necessary for people to disobey rulers when the government's laws conflicted with their religious beliefs. In colonial America, some Quakers did not pay military taxes because their religion rejected war.

In 1849, U.S. writer Henry David Thoreau helped spread the idea of civil disobedience to other groups. In his essay, "On the Duty of Civil Disobedience," Thoreau explained that people should refuse to obey the law if it is unjust. In the 1850s, people who disagreed with slavery in the United States refused to return escaped slaves. In 1872, female suffragist Susan B. Anthony tried to vote when it was illegal for women to do so, and she was arrested.

During the 1950s and 1960s, Dr. Martin Luther King Jr. advocated for civil disobedience against racial injustice in the United States. Around that same time, those against the Vietnam War also utilized civil disobedience. Some refused to register for the draft that selected men to fight in the war. Today, civil disobedience continues to be a strong tool for protest groups in the United States and beyond.

240-mile (386-km) trek to Dandi on the Arabian Sea. Twenty-four days later, on April 6, Gandhi defiantly broke the law—he scooped up a handful of salt from the shore. It was a crime not to purchase salt from the government monopoly.

Residents of India's seashore now gathered their salt from the sea. Villagers prepared their own salt. People in the cities opened their own salt centers. More Indians boycotted foreign-made cloth and picketed liquor stores. A massive number of citizens were arrested. British police used force, beating and shooting protesters. But Gandhi's followers quietly accepted the abuses and arrests. When approached by mounted police, the people laid down on the ground. The horses refused to trample the defenseless people. Their quiet compliance rendered the British powerless, and it gave strength and confidence to Indians.

By May, more than 60,000 people had been arrested. In the middle of the night on May 4, while Gandhi and his followers were camped near Dandi at Karadi, 30 armed policemen stormed their camp. They arrested Gandhi.

Bludgeoned at Dharasana

While Gandhi was in jail, satyagraha intensified. The Indian people now believed that freedom was attainable. Their first major target was the Dharasana Salt Works in Gujarat. Since Gandhi was in jail, another leader stepped forward: Sarojini Naidu. She led 2,500 protesters to the government-run salt factory approximately 150 miles (241 km) north of Bombay. As usual, the group was instructed not to use violence. When police tried to turn them back, the Indians persisted. Hundreds were arrested.

On May 21, protesters returned to the gates at Dharasana. Naidu gave an impassioned speech to the huge crowd. She cried, "Although Gandhi's body is in prison, his soul goes with you."[3] Then, the men, clad in homespun robes, lined up shoulder to shoulder in rows six or seven deep. They walked with heads held high toward a horde of approximately 400 policemen. The police bludgeoned them, one row after another, with steel-tipped clubs.

The protesters did not resist or even raise their hands to protect their

Sarojini Naidu

Sarojini Naidu (1879–1949) accompanied Gandhi on the Salt March to Dandi and then led the Dharasana Salt Works protest. This child prodigy and poet eventually became the first woman president of the INC. She was also the first woman to become governor of an Indian state—the United Provinces, now Uttar Pradesh.

heads. They simply accepted the blows and dropped to the ground. The women, led by Naidu, helped the injured get out of the way and tended to their broken skulls and shattered faces. Before the morning was over, Naidu had been arrested.

Webb Miller, a journalist for United Press, was there, along with William Shirer of the *Chicago Tribune*. Miller's eyewitness account would attract worldwide attention. It read in part:

> *Less than 100 yards away I could hear the dull impact of clubs against bodies. The watching crowds gasped, or sometimes cheered as the volunteers crumpled before the police without even raising their arms to ward off the blows.*[4]

The story was printed in newspapers around the world. The Dharasana incident became a spectacular victory for Gandhi's peaceful resistance. The movement became known as a triumph of nonviolence over armed force.

The following January, Viceroy Lord Irwin made a statement to India's Legislative Assembly:

> *No one can fail to recognize the spiritual force that impels Mr. Gandhi to count no sacrifice too great in the cause, as he believes, of the India he loves.*[5]

That month, Gandhi and other INC members were released from jail. In February and March, Gandhi and the viceroy had several meetings. The result was the Irwin-Gandhi Pact, approved on March 4, 1931. Gandhi agreed to discontinue the satyagraha movement, and the British agreed to release all prisoners arrested during the protests. The British also consented to repeal the Salt Tax. Indians could now produce salt for their own use and sell it legally.

LONDON NEGOTIATIONS

In September, Gandhi arrived in London for a roundtable conference with England's highest officials. He was there to convince the British that Indian self-rule must be established. When he walked up the stairs of the prime minister's residence, he wore only a homespun loincloth and shawl. He insisted on wearing the symbol of India's poorest citizens to visit the prime minister.

After spending 84 days in England, Gandhi returned to India.

Churchill and Gandhi

In the early 1930s, Britain's Winston Churchill openly condemned Gandhi and called him "a seditious Middle Temple lawyer, now posing as a [Hindu holy man] of a type well-known in the East, striding half-naked up the steps of the Viceregal palace."[6]

Indians had more freedom, but Britain still had
a firm hold on the country. The INC passed a
resolution to renew civil disobedience. Within three
weeks of Gandhi's return, he would be in jail once
again.

Fast Unto Death

On September 20, 1932, Gandhi began what
he called a "fast unto death."[7] He was protesting
the government's latest attempt to separate voters
according to Hindu, Muslim, and untouchables.
Gandhi's attempts to unify the people were
crumbling. The country was divided three ways.

Gandhi's fast ignited the passions of the people,
who again called for independence. Millions
fasted along with Gandhi for the first 24 hours.
On September 26, after seven days of fasting, an
agreement was reached with the British. It came
to be called the Poona or Yeravda Pact. It gave the
untouchables fair representation and other rights
in the legislature. Gandhi broke his fast and drank a
cup of orange juice. His "Epic Fast," as it came to be
called, added momentum to Gandhi's cause.

Gandhi traveled to London for a roundtable conference.

Indians protesting the arrest of Gandhi and other INC leaders lie on the ground during a tear gas attack.

INDEPENDENCE DAY

O ver the next seven years, Gandhi continued to protest British rule. Again and again, he spent time in jail. When he was not in jail, he toured India's poorest districts. At the end of 1939, World War II broke out, and the British became embroiled in worldwide conflict. For a while, Gandhi quieted his demands for independence so Britain could concentrate on defeating its enemies. But on August 8, 1942, Gandhi demanded that the British leave India. He told the people to again carry out nonviolent civil disobedience in what came to be called the Quit India Movement. He was not prepared for what would happen next.

Large-Scale Violence

Over the next 24 hours, Gandhi, Naidu, Mirabehn, and most of the INC leaders were jailed. The following day, Kasturbai was also arrested. Most of them would stay in jail for the rest of the war. In retaliation, large-scale violence broke out all over India. People burned government offices, exploded bombs, and cut off electricity. They sabotaged railroad stations, telegraph offices, and anything else related to British rule. British officials were attacked; some were killed. Workers went on strike, and thousands of people were arrested and fined. The government held Gandhi responsible.

Gandhi began writing letters to British officials, demanding rights for the Indian people. In a letter to the viceroy written January 19, 1943, Gandhi stated his firm belief in nonviolence. He explained that from jail he had no control over events outside. He held the British government responsible:

> *Of course, I deplore the happenings which have taken place since 9th August last. But have I not laid the whole blame for them at the door of the Government of India?*[1]

In February, Gandhi went on a fast to purify himself of the violence and to appeal for justice for his people.

Death of Kasturbai

Gandhi did not mind being in prison, but Kasturbai was extremely unhappy there. At the beginning of 1944, she became very ill. Gandhi knew his wife was dying and rarely left her. He sat with her for hours each day, holding her head in his lap. Their sons visited the jail whenever possible. On February 22, 1944, their youngest son, Devdas, brought his mother some holy water from the Ganges River. She drank it and said to her husband, "My death should be an occasion for rejoicing."[2] That evening, 74-year-old Kasturbai died in her husband's arms. They had been married 60 years.

Gandhi was not allowed to leave
the prison to organize his wife's
cremation, so the funeral pyre was
lit on prison grounds. Kasturbai's
death took its toll on Gandhi, and he
suffered from illness over the next
two months.

TROUBLE WITH JINNAH

On May 6, Gandhi and the other
prisoners were released. During
Gandhi's prison stay, Muslim leader
Muhammad Ali Jinnah had rallied
support to divide India and give
Muslims their own state. In his youth,
Jinnah had backed Hindu-Muslim
unity, but over time, he drifted away
from this optimistic stance. Splitting
with the Congress in the 1930s, he
advocated separate electorates for
Muslims. By 1940, with the passing
of the Lahore Resolution, he sided
firmly with those who called for
the creation of Pakistan. Now, he
opposed the Quit India Movement

Muhammad Ali Jinnah

Muhammad Ali Jinnah is
considered the founder
of Pakistan. He was first
recognized for his work
with the INC to promote
Hindu-Muslim unity. But
eventually, he joined the
All India Muslim League
and promoted a separate
state for Muslims. Jinnah
died on September 11,
1948, just over a year
after Pakistan became a
country.

and advocated a separate state for Muslims. Gandhi talked to Jinnah fourteen times in 1944, but efforts at unification failed. Gandhi rejected the thought of a divided India. It went against everything he had worked for all his life.

Through an organization called the Muslim League, Jinnah declared August 16, 1944, to be Direct Action Day. The Muslim League demanded a separate state for Muslims. Violence broke out all over India, especially in Calcutta. Large-scale riots lasted four days. Thousands were killed.

Gandhi's Call for Unity

Gandhi believed that Muslims and Hindus needed to unite and work for an independent India together. In a speech he made in August 1942, Gandhi pleaded for Muslims and Hindus to work together:

There is much in my heart that I would like to pour out before this assembly. . . . You may take it from me that it is with me a matter of life and death. If we Hindus and [Muslims] mean to achieve a heart unity, without the slightest mental reservation on the part of either, we must first unite in the effort to be free from the shackles of this empire. If Pakistan after all is to be a portion of India, what objection can there be for [Muslims] against joining this struggle for India's freedom? The Hindus and [Muslims] must, therefore, unite in the first instance on the issue of fighting for freedom. Jinnah . . . thinks the war will last long. I do not agree with him. . . . I, therefore, want freedom immediately, this very night, before dawn, if it can be had. Freedom cannot now wait for the realization of communal unity. If that unity is not achieved, sacrifices necessary for it will have to be much greater than would have otherwise sufficed.[3]

Muslim Gangs

Conflicts between Hindus and Muslims were at their height in the late 1940s. Many atrocities were committed by both Hindu and Muslim communities. But in Muslim-dominated East Bengal, Hindus were mostly on the receiving end. In October 1946, Muslim gangs in East Bengal ransacked the area and rose up against the Hindus, killing, humiliating, and torturing them. Hindu houses were set on fire, Hindu women were raped, and Hindu children were brutally murdered. India seemed on the brink of civil war.

Gandhi felt compelled to go where the violence was taking place. After stopping briefly in Calcutta, he arrived at East Bengal, where he saw the gruesome carnage. He set up his own headquarters and placed one of his followers in each village. Each leader was to provide morality and protect villagers who had survived. Gandhi's dream of a peaceful, united India was fading.

Pakistan

On June 3, 1947, Viceroy Lord Louis Mountbatten announced the establishment of Pakistan, a country set aside for Muslims. It was part

of the Indian Independence Act that
divided India into two countries and
granted independence to both. On
August 15, 1947, India and Pakistan
became independent nations. British
rule came to an end. Millions of
Muslims migrated to Pakistan and
millions of Hindus moved to India.
Where the two populations met in
the middle, there was mass mayhem,
violence, and death. Gandhi's dream
of an independent India had come
true, but it was a bittersweet victory.
He had never wanted religion to
divide the people.

Jawaharlal Nehru now became the
first prime minister of independent
India. Just before midnight on
August 14, he spoke to the Indian
people in what came to be called his
Tryst With Destiny speech:

Pakistan Today

Pakistan is located on the
northwest border of India.
Its neighbors to the west
are Afghanistan and Iran.
In the far northeast is the
Republic of China. The
country has the second
largest Muslim popula-
tion in the world, after
Indonesia. More than
170 million people live
in Pakistan, making it
the world's sixth most
populated country. India
is almost tied with Paki-
stan for the second largest
Muslim population in the
world. There are roughly
as many Muslims living
in India as there are in the
entire Middle East.

*Long years ago we made a tryst with destiny, and now the
time comes when we shall redeem our pledge. . . . At the
stroke of the midnight hour, when the world sleeps, India*

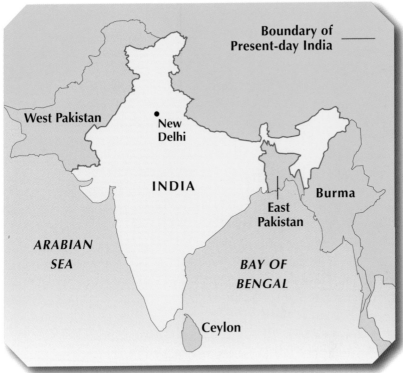

A map of independent India

will awake to life and freedom. A moment comes, which comes but rarely in history, when we step out from the old to the new, when an age ends, and when the soul of a nation, long suppressed, finds utterance.[4]

In his speech, Nehru gave credit to Gandhi:

On this day our first thoughts go to the architect of this freedom, the Father of our Nation [Gandhi], who, embodying

**First Prime Minister
of India**

On August 15, 1947, Jawaharlal Nehru became free India's first prime minister. That day, he was given the honor of raising the flag of new independent India in New Delhi. His first year of service was filled with violence as Hindus and Muslims each tried to persuade the states of Kashmir and Jammu to join their countries. This close friend of Gandhi served as India's prime minister for 18 years, until he died of a heart attack in 1964. He is known for his work with the poor and for promoting better education for children. As of 2010, he was the longest serving prime minister of India.

the old spirit of India, held aloft the torch of freedom and lighted up the darkness that surrounded us.[5]

At the end of his speech, Nehru proclaimed equality for all people of India: "All of us, to whatever religion we may belong, are equally the children of India with equal rights, privileges and obligations."[6] However, not everyone was happy about what had just occurred in India. Gandhi did not believe that independence had been truly reached yet. And not everyone would look up to Gandhi, the man Nehru called the Father of the Nation, in the future.

Jawaharlal Nehru became the first prime minister of India.

In January 1948, Gandhi fasted to help end the violence in Delhi.

ASSASSINATION
AND LEGACY

*I*n September 1947, just two weeks after
India became an independent nation,
violence erupted in Calcutta. Gandhi was there and
started another fast unto death. He would end it
"only if and when sanity returns to Calcutta."[1] Four

days later, Gandhi was very weak from not eating.
Calcutta's officials took action. They were afraid
Gandhi's death would lead to all-out revolt. So,
they sent Gandhi a written promise that peace would
return to the city. Gandhi then broke his fast.

Violence was also rampant in other places in
India. In the north, riots remained out of control.
In Delhi, the capital, thousands were killed and
multitudes injured. The situation in Delhi was
worse than in Calcutta. The dead lay in the
streets, and the hospitals were overflowing with the
wounded. Many people lashed out at Gandhi for
not performing a miracle and saving India. The
new independent nation was now on the brink of
self-destruction.

Satyagraha's Last Resort

In January 1948, Gandhi told his followers,
"I yearn for heart friendship between Hindus, Sikhs
and Muslims. . . . Today it is non-existent. . . .
Fasting is a satyagraha's last resort."[2] On January 13,
in Delhi, Gandhi began a fast that he called
"indefinite." He explained, "The fast will end when
and if I am satisfied that there is a reunion of hearts
of all communities."[3]

During the fast, disruptions took place outside his dwelling. Some Hindus and Sikhs shouted "*Gandhi mordabad*"—"Death to Gandhi"—and "Blood for blood."[4] They were protesting Hindu-Muslim unity and the help they thought Gandhi was giving the Muslims in Pakistan.

On the sixth day of his fast, Gandhi was alarmingly weak. The 78-year-old Mahatma now weighed only 107 pounds (48.5 kilograms). Fearful that India's Bapu might die, community leaders gave Gandhi their promises of peace. That day, Gandhi ended his fast and drank a glass of orange juice.

Immediately, Gandhi went back to work. He planned a march to Pakistan to unify the two countries. He also held daily prayer meetings and spoke about reconciliation. On January 30, 1948, Gandhi woke up at his usual time: 3:30 a.m. He cleaned his teeth with a stick, prayed, and then drafted part of India's new constitution. At approximately 9:30 a.m., he had breakfast: goat's milk, tomato juice, oranges, and boiled vegetables. The rest of the day was filled with writing letters and meeting with people. At approximately 5:00 p.m., Gandhi made his way across the gardens for the evening prayer meeting. Supporting him at each side were two young women from his extended family, Manubehn and Abhabehn. Still weak from the fast, he depended on them to help him walk.

Assassinated

Gandhi passed through the growing crowd that had come for prayer. One man pushed through the crowd to approach Gandhi. He bent down as if he was bowing and rose with a gun in his hand. He fired at Gandhi three times. The first shot hit Gandhi in the stomach; the other two struck him in the chest. As blood dripped down his homespun shawl, Gandhi cried out: *"Hai Rama! Hai Rama!"*—"Oh God! Oh God!"[5]

Nathuram Vinayak Godse

Gandhi's assassin, Nathuram Vinayak Godse, had idolized Gandhi when he was a boy. When Godse dropped out of high school, he joined a Hindu activist group called the Akhil Bharatiya Hindu Mahasabha (All Indian Hindu Assembly), which supported Gandhi. However, Godse and his associates later rejected Gandhi and his cause. They believed he was turning his back on Hindus in order to help Muslims and other minorities. They held Gandhi responsible for the division of India. Godse was 37 when he assassinated Gandhi.

Godse went to trial on May 27, 1948, and admitted his guilt. On November 8, 1949, Godse was sentenced to death by hanging for assassinating Gandhi. Jawaharlal Nehru, the new prime minister of India, and two of Gandhi's sons tried to get the death sentence put aside. They claimed that Gandhi would be disgraced since he opposed the death penalty. However, Godse was hanged at Ambala on November 15, 1949.

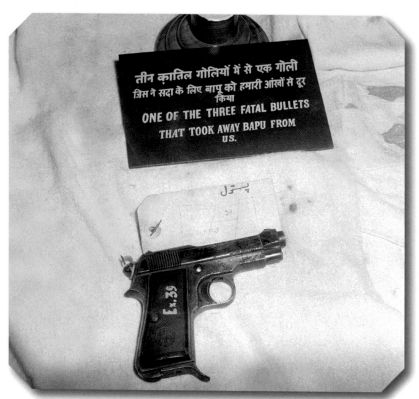

The gun Godse used to kill Gandhi is now on display in New Delhi, India.

While Gandhi lay dead on the ground, police overpowered his assassin, Nathuram Vinayak Godse. He was a Hindu and editor of an extremist Hindu newspaper in Poona. He was not alone in his assassination plot; five others were involved. Godse would hang for his crime. His conspirators would serve life sentences in prison.

The crowd was shocked. Some wept, others shouted, and many ran. Finally, after approximately ten minutes, Gandhi's body was picked up and taken to the Birla House where he had been residing. An enormous crowd gathered, pushing their way to the windows to catch a final glimpse of this man of truth and peace who had become the symbol of India.

That evening, speaking by radio from Delhi, Prime Minister Nehru told the people of India that Gandhi was dead. In a broken, sometimes tearful voice, he said:

> *Friends and comrades, the light has gone out of our lives and there is darkness everywhere. I do not know what to tell you and how to say it. Our beloved leader, Bapu as we called him, the Father of the Nation, is no more.*[6]

Nehru went on to announce the details of the cremation the next day at the Jumna River. And he encouraged people to come and pray:

> *[T]he greatest prayer that we can offer is to take a pledge to dedicate ourselves to the truth, and to the cause for which this great countryman of ours lived and for which he has died. That is the best prayer that we can offer him and his memory. That is the best prayer that we can offer to India and ourselves.*[7]

FUNERAL PROCESSION

Throughout the night, the crowd pressed on the Birla House. Finally, Gandhi's body was taken to the roof where more people could see him. The next day, Saturday, at approximately 11:00 a.m., Gandhi was lifted onto the back of a military weapons carrier. It took his body to the funeral pyre to be burned. On his forehead was a red mark called a *tilak* and around his neck was a garland of hand-spun yarn. His body had been anointed with sandalwood paste. All but his head was covered with a blanket of flower petals. Near his head, written in rose petals, were the words "Hai Rama," the last words he had spoken.

At the head of the procession were four armored cars, followed by mounted cavalrymen armed with lances. Behind the horses were troops, policemen, and a group of Gandhi's closest followers.

Death of a Son

Harilal, Gandhi's oldest son, attended his father's cremation but mingled among the crowd unrecognized. He spent that night at the home of his brother Devdas, who always loved and encouraged him. Ill with tuberculosis, Harilal died in a Bombay hospital five months later, on June 19, 1948.

The carrier with Gandhi's body followed. Nehru stood on the carrier, which was adorned with a white, green, and saffron flag—the flag of new India. Overhead, planes swooped above the scene. Police officers mingled among the massive crowd, a sea of a million people who lined the petal-strewn streets. All were trying to catch a glimpse of their Bapu, the Father of the Nation. The procession ended at the banks of the Jumna River. There, the crowd shouted, *"Mahatma Gandhi ki jai"*—"Victory to Mahatma Gandhi."[8]

THE FUNERAL PYRE

The cremation site consisted of a brick platform covered with a fine layer of sand. Nearby was a pile of sandalwood logs, a bucket of holy water from the river, and a large can of ghee, which is a clear, semi-liquid butter. There were also leaves, flowers, incense, coconuts, and camphor. Gandhi's body was lifted onto the platform and sprinkled with holy water. Then, the logs were arranged over the body. Nehru

Cremation in India

Because India's climate is so hot and humid, people are cremated within several hours after they die. Gandhi was strongly opposed to embalming, the process of preserving a corpse through the use of chemicals and oils. Therefore, his body was merely bathed in ice-cold water and displayed in its natural state at his funeral pyre.

was asked to light the funeral pyre, but he refused. Instead, Gandhi's third son, Ramdas, set it afire. As the flames ascended, the crowd roared, *"Mahatmaji amar ho gae"*—"Mahatma has become immortal."[9] It would take the rest of the night for Gandhi's body to be completely cremated.

The ashes of Mohandas Karamchand Gandhi were divided among each province of India. Small portions of his ashes were sprinkled in all the country's sacred rivers. Finally, the remaining pieces of his bones that had not burned up were gathered and strewn into the water where the Ganges, Jumna, and Saraswati rivers meet.

"Generations to come . . . will scarce believe that such a one as this ever in flesh and blood walked upon this earth."[10]

—*Albert Einstein, referring to Gandhi*

LEGACY

Over the years, memorials and statues of Gandhi have been erected throughout the world. They honor a man who lived a simple, unadorned, religious life and yet conquered the British Empire. They are a reminder that by nonviolent means, a man now known simply as Gandhi liberated a nation and changed the world.

Gandhi's body is carried through crowds of mourners to the funeral pyre.

TIMELINE

1869	1878	1880
Mohandas Karamchand Gandhi is born on October 2 in Porbandar, Gujarat, India.	Gandhi enters Taluka School in Rajkot.	Gandhi starts Kathiawar High School in Rajkot.

1891	1893	1896
Gandhi passes the Bar exam. He returns to India and learns of his mother's death.	Gandhi sails for South Africa to provide legal representation. He is kicked off a train for standing up against racial injustice.	Gandhi returns briefly to India and moves his family to South Africa.

1883

Gandhi marries
Kasturbai Makanji.

1885

Gandhi's father dies.
Gandhi's first child
dies a few days
after birth.

1888

Gandhi enters
Samaldas College but
leaves after one term.
He travels to London
to attend law school.

1904

Gandhi establishes
his first ashram,
following the
Jain principle
of aparigraha.

1907

Gandhi begins
satyagraha, nonviolent
civil disobedience,
after passage
of the Asiatic
Registration Act.

1915

Gandhi returns
to India. He tours
the country. He
establishes the
Satyagraha Ashram
at Kochrab.

TIMELINE

1919

Gandhi calls for a countrywide hartal, or strike. The government passes the Rowlatt Act, and protests follow.

1919

Thousands of Indians are massacred at Amritsar on April 13.

1920

Gandhi becomes president of the All India Home Rule League.

1932

Gandhi begins the "fast unto death" on September 20.

1942

Gandhi demands that the British quit India. He is arrested and jailed along with his wife and top followers.

1944

Gandhi's wife, Kasturbai, dies in prison on February 22. Gandhi is released from prison in May.

1921

Gandhi is arrested on March 10 and tried at the Great Trial on March 18.

1930

Gandhi declares India's independence on January 26 and begins the Salt March on March 12.

1931

The Irwin-Gandhi Pact is approved on March 4. Gandhi negotiates with British officials in London.

1947

The government establishes Pakistan for India's Muslim population and grants independence to Pakistan and India on August 15.

1948

Gandhi begins an "indefinite" fast on January 13.

1948

Gandhi is assassinated on January 30 by a Hindu extremist. Gandhi is cremated on January 31.

Essential Facts

Date of Birth
October 2, 1869

Place of Birth
Porbandar, Gujarat, India

Date of Death
January 30, 1948

Parents
Karamchand and Putlibai Gandhi

Education
Taluka School, Rajkot; Kathiawar High School, Rajkot; Samaldas College, Bhavnagar; University College, London

Marriage
Kasturbai Makanji Gandhi (May 1883)

Children
unnamed infant (1885), Harilal (1888–1948), Manilal (1892–1956), Ramdas (1897–1969), Devdas (1900–1957)

CAREER HIGHLIGHTS

Gandhi briefly worked as a lawyer and dedicated the rest of his life to social reform and simple living.

SOCIETAL CONTRIBUTION

In South Africa, Gandhi began his campaign for equal rights for Indians and other people of color. He stayed in South Africa for 21 years and established new freedoms and reduced taxes for Indians. In India, Gandhi declared satyagraha— nonviolent civil disobedience—through strikes, protests, marches, and fasts. In 1930, Gandhi declared Purna Swaraj—India's Declaration of Independence—and then defied the British government by encouraging people to make their own salt and spin and weave their own cloth. This broke the government's monopoly on two of the most profitable commodities in India.

Gandhi lived to see an independent India in 1947, but along with independence came a divided country—Pakistan and India—and a wider schism between Muslims and Hindus.

CONFLICTS

Although Gandhi's movements were meant to be nonviolent, they sometimes erupted in riots, disruptions, murders, and arrests. Gandhi himself was arrested several times. Conflicts between Muslims and Hindus also troubled Gandhi, who hoped that these religious groups could live together in peace.

QUOTE

"You must not lose faith in humanity. Humanity is an ocean; if a few drops of the ocean are dirty, the ocean does not become dirty."—*Gandhi*

ADDITIONAL RESOURCES

SELECT BIBLIOGRAPHY

Easwaran, Eknath. *Gandhi, the Man: The Story of His Transformation.* Tomales, CA: Nilgiri Press, 1997.

Fischer, Louis. *The Life of Mahatma Gandhi.* New York, NY: Harper & Row, 1950.

Gandhi, Mohandas K. *Autobiography: The Story of My Experiments With Truth.* New York, NY: Dover Publications, Inc., 1983.

Payne, Robert. *The Life and Death of Mahatma Gandhi.* New York, NY: E.P. Dutton & Co., Inc., 1969.

Wolpert, Stanley. *Gandhi's Passion: The Life and Legacy of Mahatma Gandhi.* Oxford, England: Oxford University Press, 2001.

FURTHER READING

Furbee, Mary, and Mike Furbee. *Mohandas Gandhi.* San Diego, CA: Lucent Books, 2000.

Kudlinski, Kathleen. *Gandhi: Young Nation Builder.* New York, NY: Aladdin Paperbacks, 2006.

Levi, Primo. *Gandhi.* London, England: DK Children, 2006.

Nicholson, Michael. *Mahatma Gandhi.* Farmington Hills, MI: Blackbirch Press, 2003.

Web Links

To learn more about Mahatma Gandhi, visit ABDO Publishing Company online at **www.abdopublishing.com**. Web sites about Mahatma Gandhi are featured on our Book Links page. These links are routinely monitored and updated to provide the most current information available.

Places To Visit

Gandhi Memorial Center
4748 Western Avenue, Bethesda, MD 20816
301-320-6871
www.gandhimemorialcenter.org
The Gandhi Memorial Center spreads the philosophy, ideals, life, service, and teachings of Gandhi, as well as the cultural heritage of India.

Mahatma Gandhi Memorial
Washington, DC
www.indianembassy.org/gandhi
Located across the street from the Embassy of India, the memorial plaza and bronze statue honor Gandhi's long marches, his simplicity, his philosophy of nonviolence, and his commitment to world peace.

Glossary

ashram
　　A place of religious retreat for Hindus.

bar examination
　　An exam required to become a lawyer, proving that one is qualified to practice law.

betrothal
　　A mutual promise to marry; an engagement.

Buddhist
　　A follower of the Buddhist religion and the teachings of Buddha.

caste system
　　A social system of dividing the population into groups based on heredity and profession.

chastity
　　A condition of being pure, virtuous, and usually virginal.

Christian
　　A follower of a Christian religion who believes in Jesus Christ as savior and follows his teachings.

Hindu
　　A follower of Hinduism, characterized by belief in reincarnation and a supreme being of many forms.

homespun
　　Plain, coarse cloth made of yarn spun and woven by hand.

illiterate
　　Unable to read and write.

Jain
> A follower of Jainism, which teaches the immortality of the soul and denies the existence of a supreme being.

Muslim
> A follower of Islam, a religion characterized by submission to Allah and to Muhammad as the greatest and last prophet of God.

pacifist
> A person who believes that disputes should and can be settled peacefully.

penance
> An act of self-punishment to show repentance and sorrow for a sin or wrongdoing.

puppet ruler
> A ruler chosen by a larger government official to oversee a government and who is controlled by that larger government.

pyre
> A heap of flammable material for burning a corpse as a funeral rite.

tryst
> An agreement to meet at a certain time and place.

viceroy
> The governor of a country or province who represents a monarch, such as a king or a queen.

SOURCE NOTES

Chapter 1. The Salt March
1. Gandhi and Dennis Dalton. *Mahatma Gandhi.* Indianapolis, IN: Hackett Publishing Company, 1996. 72.
2. "Salt Tax." *Mahatma Gandhi. Young India, 1919–1922.* New York, NY: B.W. Huebsch, 1924. Quoted in Stanley Wolpert. *Gandhi's Passion: The Life and Legacy of Mahatma Gandhi.* Oxford, England: Oxford University Press, 2001. 143.
3. Gandhi and Dennis Dalton. *Mahatma Gandhi.* Indianapolis, IN: Hackett Publishing Company, 1996. 72.
4. "Gandhi Labels British Rule in India 'A Curse.'" *Chicago Daily Tribune.* 7 Mar. 1930. 8 Jul. 2009 <http://pqasb.pqarchiver.com/chicagotribune/access/458880572.html?dids=458880572:45888 0572&FMT=CITE&FMTS=CITE:AI&date=Mar+07%2C+1930&author=&pub=Chicago+Tribune&desc=GANDHI+LABELS+BRITISH+RULE+IN+INDIA+%22A+CURSE%22&pqatl=google>.
5. "Draft Declaration for January 26, 1930." *Collected Works of Mahatma Gandhi.* vol. 81. Ahmedabad: Navajivan Trust, July 17– October 31, 1945. 319. Quoted in Stanley Wolpert. *Gandhi's Passion: The Life and Legacy of Mahatma Gandhi.* Oxford, England: Oxford University Press, 2001. 141–142.
6. "Penal Sections of the Salt Act (Dated 1882)." *The Salt March: 75 Years.* 8 Jul. 2009 <http://www.saltmarch.org.in/h_daterecord.html>.

Chapter 2. Timid Beginnings
1. Louis Fischer. *The Life of Mahatma Gandhi.* New York, NY: Harper & Row, 1950. 13.
2. Mohandas K. Gandhi. *Autobiography: The Story of My Experiments with Truth.* New York, NY: Dover Publications. Inc., 1983. 2.
3. Robert Payne. *The Life and Death of Mahatma Gandhi.* New York, NY: E.P. Dutton & Co., Inc., 1969. 29.
4. Ibid. 26.
5. Louis Fischer. *The Life of Mahatma Gandhi.* New York, NY: Harper & Row, 1950. 15.

Chapter 3. Child Marriage

1. "Seven Vows of Marriage." *Indian Weddings*. 30 Jul. 2009 <http://weddings.iloveindia.com/indian-weddings/seven-vows.html>.
2. Mohandas K. Gandhi. *Autobiography: The Story of My Experiments with Truth*. New York, NY: Dover Publications, Inc., 1983. 6.
3. Ibid. 41.
4. Ibid. 42.

Chapter 4. The Pain of Prejudice

1. Mohandas K. Gandhi. *Autobiography: The Story of My Experiments with Truth*. New York, NY: Dover Publications, Inc., 1983. 153.

Chapter 5. Massacre at Amritsar

1. Eknath Easwaran. *Gandhi, the Man: The Story of His Transformation*. Tomales, CA: Nilgiri Press, 1997. 148.
2. Nigel Collett. *The Butcher of Amritsar: General Reginald Dyer*. London: Hambledon Continuum, 2007. 344.
3. Ibid. 262.
4. Louis Fischer. *The Life of Mahatma Gandhi*. New York, NY: Harper & Row, 1950. 179.
5. John F. Burns. "India and England Beg to Differ; Tiptoeing Through the Time of the Raj." *New York Times*. 19 Oct. 1997. 10 Aug. 2009 <http://www.nytimes.com/1997/10/19/weekinreview/india-and-england-beg-to-differ-tiptoeing-through-the-time-of-the-raj.html?sec=&spon=&pagewanted=all>.
6. Ibid.
7. Nigel Collett. *The Butcher of Amritsar: General Reginald Dyer*. London: Hambledon Continuum, 2007. 262.

Source Notes Continued

Chapter 6. Homespun

1. Louis Fischer. *The Life of Mahatma Gandhi.* New York, NY: Harper & Row, 1950. 189.
2. Ibid.
3. Mahatma Gandhi. *All Men Are Brothers: Autobiographical Reflections.* New York, NY: Continuum, 2005. 100.
4. Louis Fischer. *The Life of Mahatma Gandhi.* New York, NY: Harper & Row, 1950. 210.
5. Ibid. 200–201.
6. Ibid. 202–203.
7. Ibid. 475.

Chapter 7. The Power of Salt

1. Louis Fischer. *The Life of Mahatma Gandhi.* New York, NY: Harper & Row, 1950. 223.
2. Ibid. 267.
3. Webb Miller. "Natives Beaten Down by Police in India Salt Bed Raid." 21 May, 1930. *100 Years of Journalistic Excellence.* UPI Archives. 14 Aug. 2009 <http://100years.upi.com/sta_1930-05-21.html>.
4. Ibid.
5. Ranbir Vohra. *The Making of India: A Historical Survey.* Armonk, NY: M.E. Sharpe, 2000. 151.
6. Alex Von Tunzelmann. *Indian Summer: The Secret History of the End of an Empire.* New York, NY: Henry Holt and Company, 2008. 90.
7. Louis Fischer. *The Life of Mahatma Gandhi.* New York, NY: Harper & Row, 1950. 306.

Chapter 8. Independence Day

1. Mohandas Karamchand Gandhi and V. Geetha, Ed. *Soul Force: Gandhi's Writings on Peace.* Chennai, India: Tara Books, 2004. 342.

2. Robert Payne. *The Life and Death of Mahatma Gandhi.* New York, NY: E.P. Dutton & Co., Inc., 1969. 503.

3. Mahatma Gandhi. "The 'Quit India' Speeches." *Mahatma Gandhi Information.* 10 Feb. 2010 <http://www.gandhi-mainbhavan.org/gandhicomesalive/speech6.htm>.

4. Jawaharlal Nehru. "Tryst With Destiny." *Internet Modern History Sourcebook.* Fordham University, 1998. 18 Aug. 2009 <http://www.fordham.edu/halsall/mod/1947nehru1.html>.

5. Ibid.

6. Ibid.

Chapter 9. Assassination and Legacy

1. Homer A. Jack, Ed. *The Gandhi Reader: A Sourcebook of His Life and Writings, Volume I.* New York, NY: Grove Press, 1994. 442.

2. Stanley Wolpert. *Gandhi's Passion: The Life and Legacy of Mahatma Gandhi.* Oxford, England: Oxford University Press, 2001. 253.

3. Ibid.

4. Robert Payne. *The Life and Death of Mahatma Gandhi.* New York, NY: E.P. Dutton & Co., Inc., 1969. 561.

5. Ibid. 590.

6. Jawaharlal Nehru. *Independence and After: A Collection of Speeches, 1946–1949.* Manchester, NH: Ayer Company Publishers, 1971. 18.

7. Ibid. 19.

8. Robert Payne. *The Life and Death of Mahatma Gandhi.* New York, NY: E.P. Dutton & Co., Inc., 1969. 597.

9. Ibid. 598.

10. Harold G. Coward. *Indian Critiques of Gandhi.* New York, NY: State University of New York Press, 2003. 107.

INDEX

ABOUT THE AUTHOR

Sue Vander Hook has been writing and editing books for nearly 20 years. Although her writing career began with several nonfiction books for adults, Sue's main focus is educational books for children and young adults. She especially enjoys writing about historical events and the biographies of people who made a difference. Her published works include a high school curriculum and series on disease, technology, and sports. Sue lives with her family in Mankato, Minnesota.

PHOTO CREDITS

Elliott & Fry/Getty Images, cover, 3; AP Images, 6, 23, 24, 34, 65, 75, 85, 90, 96 (bottom); Mansell/Time & Life Pictures/Getty Images, 9; Red Line Editorial, 13, 14, 83; Lindsay Hebberd/ Corbis, 17; Henry Guttmann/Getty Images, 21, 29, 96 (top); Ansell/Time & Life Pictures/Getty Images, 33, 97; Hulton Archive/ Getty Images, 43; Popperfoto/Getty Images, 44, 56, 66, 99 (top); Branger/Roger Viollet/Getty Images, 49; Bettmann/Corbis, 50; John Moore/AP Images, 55; Hulton Archive/Getty Images, 60; Keystone/Getty Images, 76, 98; Staff/Desfor/AP Images, 86; Max Desfor/AP Images, 95, 99 (bottom)